I WAS A SHIPWRECK SCHOLAR

SCHOLAR

POEMS ON LOSS, RECKONING, AND WONDER

GREGORY LeSTAGE

JPZ
J. P. Zenger Books

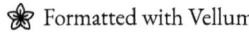

To my mother
Karolyn Linda LeStage

We must have
the stubbornness to accept our gladness in the ruthless
furnace of this world.

— JACK GILBERT, "A BRIEF FOR THE DEFENSE"

There is a pleasure in the pathless woods,
There is a rapture on the lonely shore,
There is society where none intrudes,
By the deep Sea, and the music in its roar:
I love not Man less, but Nature more

— LORD BYRON, "CHILDE HAROLD'S PILGRIMAGE"

Contents

WONDER

PREFACE

I am a poet of place.

My place is Cape Cod, the flexed arm of Massachusetts that curls 65 miles north into the Atlantic Ocean. This glacially sculpted, low-lying, sandy peninsula is characterized by outwash plains, dunes, and cliffs. Its waters are ocean, bays, and kettle ponds. Its materials are sand and gravel.

Although geologically young, humans – both Wampanoags and white – have continuously lived here longer than most other parts of the country. Although the land is dynamic and fragile, the people inhabiting it for centuries are change resistant and hardy. My identity and sensibility are intertwined with the living symbiosis of the physical, historical, social, and familial realities of this place. Wind, tide, and salt are constantly at work on the coastline and on me.

I am drawn to the New England Realist tradition that contemplates moral and physical geography, history, inheritance, and labor with emotional gravity and elevated plain speech. Here in me are Robert Frost, Donald Hall, Galway Kinnell, and Richard Wilbur. I am drinking from and swimming in their waters.

This collection studies the forces that shape a life: time, nature, human connection. Time warps memory; memory distorts time. The natural world, especially the sea and what is at its edges, becomes the sublime when we immerse in it. Connection, especially with family, finds meaning as forcefully through loss as it does through love. Weightlessness takes meaning from the experience of bearing great weight.

It also explores the power of loss and the restorative effects of coping and hoping when faced with it. It gives the same embrace to impermanence and isolation as it does to immovable truths and human kinship. The belief is that the loss of time, nature, and love induces transformation fueled by hope, a renewable energy. Hope is a story set in the future in which we're a character, safe and sound.

Stories also provide the rationale for what was. As the *New Yorker's* Adam Gopnick observed:

> We have merely a self-deluding, 'narrating self,' one that recites obviously tendentious stories, shaped by our evolutionary history to help us cope with life [...] We are made up of stories – and we make them up.

Oliver Sacks, too, wrote about his hit-and-miss efforts to make meaning out of the swirl of things. In a private letter to his friend, the philosopher Hugh Moorhead, he describes how his cycle of reckoning with the elusiveness of meaning is driven by loss and wonder. His vast array of writing – his storytelling – embodies this philopsophy:

> I do not, at least consciously, have a steady sense of life's meaning. I keep losing it, and having to re-achieve it, again and again. I can only re-achieve – or remember – it when I am inspired by things or events or people, when I get a sense of the immense intricacy and mystery, but also the deep ordering positivity, of Nature and History [...] I do not believe in, never have believed in, any transcendental spirit above Nature; but there is a spirit in Nature, a cosmogenic spirit, which commands my respect and love; and it is this, perhaps most deeply, which serves to explain life, give it meaning.

This collection reflects Sacks' notion of uncertainty wrapped in certainty, or vice versa, in its three sections – loss, reckoning, and wonder. One poem is not reliant on the ones that proceed it. Each should stand on its own. However, there is a thematic progression, or movement, that follows an arc from beginning to end: what happens to us, how we come to terms with it, and the marvels that help us rise above all of it.

Why poetry? Because, for me, it's the literary form best suited to sending flares of beauty, however unrefined or simple they are. There is beauty in the finding of it during the writing process; also in the end state when it is revealed.

~

Poets, critics, and scholars have been writing about poetry's demise since the middle of the 19th century. Industrialization, realism, secularization, and societal fragmentation assailed it during that century and into the next. Then mass media and the dominance of the novel threatened to quash it. Academic elitism made it abstract and confined it to universities and salons. By the turn of this century, it had become a subculture disconnected from mainstream readership and public discourse.

Today, reports of its decline continue. Over the past twenty-five years, and especially in the last ten, many have documented the slow, steady dissipation of formal or "literary" poetry from school and university curricula, as well as from the non-digital public domain. Small poetry presses, long a vessel for the art, have disappeared under the pressure of unsustainable economics, distributor collapse, and reduced public grant support. It is a form of exclusion, be it intentional or unintentional. With the vanishing forums go the mediating voices, the teachers, the standard bearers.

However, and meanwhile, evidence of a recovery in – or because of – the digital domain is abundant. Its virtual presence has expanded exponentially; the internet has democratized the art. Everyone can find or create a platform to be, or appear as, a poet. The inclusion of voices, which is a good and necessary thing, enabled by the low-to-no bar of self-publishing and the internet's open borders and land grab has enlarged the environment in which poetry exists.

So, between decline and recovery we can see where poetry is and is not living. From a topographical perspective, it looks like habitat change – with both losses and gains affecting the form itself.

Increasingly, the chosen form is the formless or, rather, the form is the performative space in which the performer often sets the rules. Also, so much written today is shaped to look like a poem on the page, but under quick examination is prose chopped up into lines and stanzas to appear like a poem, without many of the qualities that earn it that label.

I will stop here and will not wade into the century-old debate about what is versus what is not poetry. I will put a toe in, though: some of the forces shaping poetry today have thrown my own views into relief – made clear why it interests me as a form over other literary genres. It is the formal qualities that inspire me, including when choosing to ignore them.

What happens when intentionally working with the spatial, visual, audial, and temporal attributes of form? When the templates of its formal history and traditions, like rhyme and meter, inform the work? The challenge presented by poetry's relative constraints draws me in. Poetry thrives in small spaces on a page and is thin on a bookshelf; much is left to wide margins and thick novels. The eye can take it in on the page, see its shape. It is meant for the ear's brief attention, which can hear it like a song for a few minutes while listening for patterns and expecting an end. For the reader, its temporal footprint is small. Much of its power can come from ellipsis, from what is not written, which is an ultimate form of constraint.

This *condition of brevity* in an effective poem causes an inversion: from single lines it expands us geometrically. Often the expansion starts with a surprise, the spark of which can come from fire-striking one word against another, or from connecting two unexpected lines to create the hum of a current. This is a unique effect of poetry: much from little. Also, the better poetry is not fleeting. The poet wrote it to last, and it lasts, like a pilot light, in the reader.

The intent is not to attempt a unique perspective. Others have expounded on these qualities at far greater length and to great effect. Nor is it to bemoan change, quiet voices, or quash experimentation. The yin and yan of whatever forces are affecting poetry in any given era are both essential and constant. The intent is to cast these qualities in relief against the intensely and purposely momentary structure and nature of internet media, which is still a relatively new phenomenon. It is literally designed not to last. It rewards ephemera. In the background, it is training our brains to quickly dispense with what's now for what's next. Every 3 to 20 seconds. Ephemera is the reward.

Adapt to habitat change or vanish. Both have costs.

East Orleans, October 2025

LOSS

What we carry, we mourn.

I Was a Shipwreck Scholar

I was a shipwreck scholar.
I studied the forces and causes behind them.
The gales and fogs and shifting shoals.
Their captains' names, the number of lost souls.
When the life savers failed and breeches buoys fell short.

From coffee table books about ships that went down,
from library lectures in town,
I learned where to find them.
My grandfather taught me
about the *Sparrow-Hawk*, the *Whydah Gally*,
their beam and draft,
the cargo and spoils of the *General Greene*
he had seen blown ashore.
He expected wrecks
    – Twice a winter month back in the day –
and played among them like a castaway.
    When I was a boy in summer,
    I'd escape to the outermost beach
    and make camp in the deck house
    of the wrecked schooner, Montclair.

I told myself there were mooncussers in my bloodline,
made up ancestral surfmen proud
in the keepership of their stations.
Heard them all hearing the sounds
of the stripping sails slatting above the surf's roar,
of the towering breakers wracking the hulls into salvage.
Heard them telling their tales of tossed up sailors
holed up with firewood and flares
in charity houses along the shoreline.
Thought about them thinking of the sands
shaming the hulks into skeletons in a slow scour
and closeting them out of sight.

I was born too late in the century,

too far from wood, canvas, and compass;
and well on the other side of iron and radar.
The disasters had simply stopped;
Life Saving Stations fell into private hands,
became vacation homes
for those who would never need saving;
untended lighthouses formed cataracts,
went dark, became Bed & Breakfasts.

So, from the easy safety of houses
overlooking the bay and sea,
I had to settle for soft bliss,
for being kept even by the gimbals
of imagination and ignorance.
I learned enough from day camps and catboats,
from craft classes elbow deep in driftwood,
dead and dried creatures, and Elmer's glue,
and was secure in the smell of low tide and bluefish.
The dusty miller reliably quivered in gray
while pinhead mollusks clung dutifully to the spartina,
and fleets of periwinkles inched the shoreline
while wild violets speckled the myrtle
in the yard above the cove
and put their blue on my mother's blouse
and in the rainy-day-paint-by-numbers flowers
that I never finished
because the clouds would clear,
and I'd return to the pitch pines and barrens,
to the sassafras and sweet fern.

In going on to do what I was duty-bound to do
in schools and jobs, at desks and at anchor,
I came to learn that childhood was the ship that never made it,
to accept that I was wrecked
for having thrived in four dimensions –
for having seen the unseeable, rapturous colors
at either end of the rainbow,
for having heard the thunder's octaves
below and above the ear's reach,
for having lived in the stories

where I tasted the drowned in the ocean's salt,
felt the skin of the savers and the saved in the sand,
smelled the wood gone to one with the water.

THE PAST BOY

Now the flagging and dwindling that comes
from seeing children's eyes seeing
what was once seen through his own,
their bodies tensing and loosening,
building their enchantments in the current of the moment.

Feeling the past boy shrinking inside the man.
Hearing the held strength
duning his sands, leeching his soil.
Seeing the cedar of himself,
whose tallness attracted the axe and saw, the devouring beetle,
buckle and wilt under the stroke and gnaw.

Letting the dreamer go.
That boy of solitude with odd attachments,
that water-watcher, that tide-tracker
who drop-lined into wishing coves,
like into dreams in afternoons
when work at the farm garden finished early,
his hands black with the tomatoed earth and a tiny wage,
his mind turning stones, dropping the hook just so,
his bare feet printing out his manifesto
in a shoreline wander.

A Boy of Clay

At sunrise, she stood naked at the foot of a hotel bed
in front of a window framing the Matterhorn.
She was in shadow, the peak bent in the light.

He sprawled out before her ecstatic and dead.
The bedsheets vined around him, torn
in his fall from a misread height.

She who pushed him left his body there.
Her shadow whispered,
You're a toppled Roman bust.

I'm just a boy of clay, he didn't dare
say and left that to be inferred
from the scattered shards of trust.

WHAT SHOULD HAVE LASTED

Those whom we love and lose are no longer where they were before.
They are now wherever we are.
— St. John Chrysostom

It should have been the family that lasted.
It should have been my grandmother,
her fine fingers fanned out and touching everyone,
like high-tensile wire holding the bridge up, until they were not.
My great uncle shot himself on Labor Day
when we were all next door
to save us from the biting gnarl of a man he would have become
once the arthritis vined through him.
My father exited early; some will not visit his headstone,
are still looking expectantly at the door.
Stevie suffocated on a piece of meat,
others meted out their own suffocation in long marriages.

And I kept on with the keeping, with the keptness of it all,
with pursuing the secrets of blood:
how it flows, pools, clots,
how it holds intra-cellular conversations with itself.
It was an important love, but without a soft kernel.
The dominion and all the assets are safe,
except the ones with value.

It is the houses and the land that remain.
And the two towns.
Attleboro lasted after the Blizzard of '78.
The new ranch houses reemerged after the melt
sneering at the sloughing Victorians
then getting their own in foreclosure when the mall came in.
Not Aunt Helen and Uncle George,
but their Yankee accent and rattling laugh,
like a beer can with a marble in it.
The forearm-thick wysteria ruling my aunt's porch while,

out back, some other uncle slowly aged away
from being a collector of objects
to a being
around whom objects gather.

When I was a boy, I visited the industrial museum in town
to study the old machinery displayed in pieces,
body parts of beasts extinct and unreplaced,
the creator gone without a trace,
except for the name on a plaque.
A god covertly forsaking a church and leaving a note.

Old Bill when he had to give up hunting.
His feral opinions,
once antlered and slipping the cull in the pines,
now tame and listless.

The big family Christmas slowly getting smaller and less dressy,
people not bothering with gifts.
And then the big barn finally came down.

Orleans holds against the rising sea
when we plant the bluffs and expect the roots to hold the soil.

I am pulling the little red wagon of this through the streets
of Avignon and Oxford; Boston and Orleans.
Coming of age in the Alps
with a woman nearly twice my age.
The people I came to know there did not last,
and I released each girlfriend into the wild.
The dunes slow crawl grain by grain.
The snow comes and goes.
But the cobblestones and brick sidewalks hold.

Churchless, the mind sifts through the life's liturgy,
cannot find the formularies, writes its own bibles.
Puzzles over the spectral smudge on the X-ray.
I see a spirit but cannot confirm it is mine
because it never stops moving.
What is not moving is the ground I share

with all those who did not last,
is the sediment of them slowly turning into stone.
All of it worthy of etching.

I Hear My Father in the Meadow Now

I hear my father in the meadow now
pleading with the milkweed
to ready for the monarch
that no longer arrives.

He is grumbling *I told you so*
about the unsowed seed,
the fade of the meadowlark,
and the dying in the hives.

A hawk pilots a doom loop overhead.
In a moment, the mole's;
in the meadowless future, his.
The rising sea dozes the primal wrack line.

In the inert is the watershed.
New depths were once old shoals.
The what should be is not the what is.
The bittersweet twines and chokes the pine.

Beauty is fleet but slow seeming,
he used to say.
So we scattered his bonedust to slow it down,
to alchemy the soil for redeeming
and await some judgment day.

Whale Fall

We first saw it from far across the inlet
as a glinting island of fire agate,
but as our boat approached its shores
it became an archipelago of skinless flesh
in orange mounds glowing and stenching
in the December sun.

It surely died out in the open ocean.
The tidal bulge, fattened by the hungry moon
and emboldened by some autumn storm,
must have rushed it in only to maroon
it in the shallow marsh,
depriving us all of its right to a fall.

Down it should have sunk in a graceful spiral,
deflating into songlessness,
a dirge singing itself into the abyss
through fathoms of descending verses,
delivering itself as bounty to the very bottom,
where the sixgills and hagfish, eelpouts and brittle stars,
worms and snails and shrimp
in their rolling and forever feast
would turn it into lipids and sulphides,
nutrients and minerals
from which new reefs would rise
and give breath to the sea.

THE RIVER OTTERS

after Wendell Berry

When I had finally convinced myself
that there were no concerns growing in me for the world,
no worries for what my life and my children's lives may be,
I woke one night to sweet sounds of chirping in the walls
and heard them as the peace of wild things harboring in my house,
and I rested in the grace of the world.

Days later, we found two river otters in the root cellar
nestled together on the earthen floor,
like a pair of worn-out shoes,
soles up and dead,
and I was stricken
by the loss of creatures
who moved with such grace in their world,
porpoising and diving, loping and sliding in the flow of things,
and later, dawningly,
by having mistaken what I heard for what I needed,
a caterwaul for a song.

BATS DAZZLING BLACKLY

That long time ago
just after nightfall

standing in the wind
in the bygone sheep pasture
anchoring my feet
in the shallow grass
at the shelf of the bay
by the shoal of the town

looking over at the old white farmhouse
one naked spotlight burning on the outside peak
inking a geometry of shadows where it does not reach
throwing into relief where it does

      the rounded green gleam of the '49 Chevy
      the slightly swinging tracery of the rope hammock
      the billowing sag of the crab net left leaning

watching the bats dazzling blackly
through the drapery of light

hearing the oars and oarlocks
of a rowboat going back and forth
down in Cedar Cove
and the breezy voices carrying themselves up to me

all beaconed dimly
      but enough
through the dappled sorrow of all the years that followed

WHAT NOT TO BE BRILLIANT AT

There are acts that you do not want
to be brilliant at,
like last words in hostage negotiations,
writing your own obituary,
toasting to divorce.
Like eulogies for young suicides,
when whatever you have so
lushly, achingly, utterly
marshaled into words,
each one obeying the deepest meaning you assigned to it,
and even gaining whole new meanings because of
the very marshaling,
and the whole place
is swaying with the wind you are summoning,
and they are all believing one new thing
and are tribed together because of it in that one shared space
and, later, when each of us is in bed alone
we whisper some version of
waste
to ourselves,
and so begins its slow tarnish,
because how could it be otherwise?

HOUSE BEAUTIFUL

If you were ever there for a party,
but only long enough to see the splendid facades,
you believed that there were no disputes
under that roof –
the London designer worked
with the yin of the classic New England Victorian
and the yang of modern composition.

Hardwood here, hardwood there.
Muted this, matte that.
Palette coordinated, textures harmonized.
Lines of sight clean, negative space allowed for.
Furniture angled yet inviting.
Painted portraits of ancestors,
chummy photographs with famous people.
And the wallpaper quaintly hand-blocked
in Yorkshire by some octogenarian.

The communion of everything outside.
The sturdy mansard and all those chimneys.
The pristine woodpile.
The birdsong on cue in spring.
The fallen leaves arranging themselves in the October wind.

A glossy brochure in three dimensions,
a diorama at scale.

But a domestic Damascus, the siege unseen.
The soft, invisible violence of the oppressed space.
The dawn shelling from the alcove,
sniper fire from the pantry at dusk,
rockets launched in the dark from the kitchen up the stairs.
Missiled words, heat-seeking and indiscriminate.

Terror through infrastructure.
Topics stopped at checkpoints, held in blockade.
Pock marked silences, cratered conversations.

The mangled rebar of memory
and rewriting of history.

Not deprived of electricity or food,
only of power and nourishment;
not searching for wood fuel in the wreckage,
only for solace out by the woodpile.

And then the uprising.
The moment opens like a new door.

But the Checks Kept Coming In

If the mind is like a hall in which thought is like a voice speaking,
the voice is always that of someone else.
— Wallace Stevens, "Adagia"

You had the look and the size.
Your gait suggested you were going places;
people told you so and followed.
You took orders from your bloodlines
and maybe mapped the whole campaign out
or maybe planned to go on instinct
without horses or machines;
you do not recall.

You were diligent about going to the barbershop
to stay looking sharp,
to conceal the caverning inside
and then the cavern's sound,
the *plink* without an echo.
While outside
the dusking and then the stalled dusk.
Yet you always had the contract to hand,
counter-signed.

The clothes you were wearing you did not recognize,
but they fit beautifully.
And your bedsheets smelled familiar,
although you could not place the source.
But the checks kept coming in.

You performed the disappearing act
with utter perfection for years;
no one knew you were gone.
As you uninhabited the scene,
you checked for evidence
of what you left behind
and found nothing.

The Knife Drawer

She became the kind of woman
that made a man want to be alone,

to seek the easy company of the barman
in half-lit places where he wasn't known.

She a darkener of all the doorways
into him,

an anarchist in the hallways
of his reason

a rummager in the closets
of his conscience,

a picker of pockets
for his loose change of heart.

His approach to it all, to the chore,
a blind hand reaching into someone else's knife drawer.

THE SHOOK BABY

When your teacup campaigns
spilled untruth on the regular,
every ear an amphitheater
to be filled with facts bent to feelings,
with tales of teacup wars in your hinterlands
funded by your jars of pennies
collected for every sleight,

we could only conclude
that you were one of those babies
that was shaken for years
out of sight and earshot,
the shaker unknown,
even to you.
An addling in secret.

Your hands can't stop gripping
the narrow shoulders of a petty indiscretion,
the flaccid neck of a little trouble,
an offhand remark in its infancy
and shaking.

You cannot soothe the nation
of yourself.

YOU WERE

an everything trumping a nothing,
a forever trading with a never
and profiting handsomely before losing it all;

a circus that came to town and stayed
to fight for the rights
of contortionists and bears on bicycles;

an absinthe swirl in a jeweled goblet
when tap water in a mug would have sufficed,
but provided no inspiration;

an onslaught in ghost-colored skin,
whose paranormal entrances and exits
were made for stage or screen, but never cast;

a cardiogram of confidence and self-doubt –
the peak and plunge, the soar and dive,
and the space between heartbeats left empty
by your bloodline;

eight knuckles tattooed with l-o-v-e and f-e-a-r
that caressed and struck with matched passion
in a one-two combination;

an emporium of intimacy and taboo,
with open shelves and locked cabinets
richly stocked and labeled *Please Do and Do Not Touch;*

an arson with matchstick thoughts,
kerosene breath, and strike-strip tongue
when all must burn to renew or cease;

fresh-baked *pi*, whose transcendence implies
that it was impossible for either of us to solve
the ancient challenge of squaring your circle.

ON BECOMING A PHOTOGRAPH

He is now that photograph she just removed
from the face of her fridge,
its turned back slightly cold to her touch,
its face thrown down in the snowdrift
of receipts and bills
to await the morgue of the desk drawer or
cremation from the match.

On that fridge, a magnet still clings
to a cut-out recipe for something they had hoped to make together
one day in the distant future
once they had gathered all of the ingredients,
available nowhere.

The Kingmaker's Glass

The ancient Persians made big decisions by discussing them twice:
once while drunk, once while sober.
— Herodotus, *The Histories*, Book I

The stiff drink at night – that reliable
kingmaker perched dutifully at his side –
makes itself cold and indispensable,
quickens to ply and flatter, stirring pride,

secures his crowning -- then turns Svengali:
corrupts his rule, sows revolt in the court
of his faculties, its deft puppetry
a short performance of a reign cut short,

but in the kitchen readies the strong pot
so he will smell the coffee on waking –
the breath of the desperate who will plot
the arc of his rise to power; a king

-sized bed and an armchair, the grave and throne;
the false glass, the true mug, and him alone.

RECKONING

Be patient toward all that is unsolved in your heart and try to love the questions themselves.
RILKE

The Kinship of Freefall

Something there is that doesn't love a wall,
That wants it down.
— Robert Frost

The stone wall was always there
cleaving the field in two
between the old road and the woods,
slowly succumbing
to the suck of the soil
and to the forest of black locust trees that rose around it,
while their roots carried out a silent sunder from below
     one stone at a time, it seemed, over a century
to implicate us as the topplers of some rock-boned colossus,
the mostly buried spine its only remains.

After the fleam and gullet of the saws
worked their angles and valleys in the trunks,
and the trees came down in jackstraws,
we bent our backs and crow bars,
broke shovels, broke the green grip of what cloyed to the stones,
set fire to all that was not birthed as magma from the earth's mantle.
We brought machines in and fresh men.
We trucked boulders from the local quarry
to fill holes and gaps.

What we rebuilt served nothing
but the brute joy of rebuilding,
the serenity of the mindless,
because there is really nothing to divide,
nothing to keep in or out
at this stage in our lives.

It is now a task without end.
There I still am in the August swelter
gamely piling up stony permanence
while the ants succeed in the interstices,

27

and the cicadas rail in the red maples
about the brevity of it all.

Years ago, I saved a seal carcass from the beach
and buried it at the field's edge
to let nature perform its subtraction.
I will dig it up after some spring thaw
and wire the bones together and hang it
so that it moves with the breeze off the bay
like a seal remembering itself.

The lone stone dreaming of the wall,
the single bone of the body,
the word of the book,
the kinship of freefall
when it all must stop working
in order to work again.

Renting a Hopper House

Some day, I will rent a house
that Edward Hopper painted
for the sunlight and shadow,
rectangles and squares.
For the constancy of angles,
for the geometry of emptiness.

The spaces and objects will be plain
to redress the ornateness of my being.
There will be no curves or arches
to mislead my eye into feelings of calmness.
Nothing circular to suggest completeness.

Colors, like his deliberate deep greens and intense blues,
will merely serve light and shadow,
not the other way around.

Even the way my elbows will bend
when I hold my head in my hands
at the simple table
will affirm the rectilinear,
will assert their function over the beauty
of whatever it is I will be feeling
in those moments.

All gazes cast by the women
will point down or away from me.
We will appear as if something just happened
or is about to.

I will have plumbed
these isolated instants of composition
by the time my lease is up.
I won't renew.
I will have re-drafted the architecture
of an inner life vast and varied,

unconcerned with where I might be placed
in relation to the arrangements of color, form, and design.

Over Our Fathers

after Robert Hayden

We never get over our fathers,
and we're not required to.
— Irish Proverb

My father left the house before sunrise,
seven days a week, it seemed.
He'd wake me to drink
Carnation Instant Breakfast mixed with milk
together in the mostly dark kitchen before driving off in his Chevy
to be with his other family,
his workers at the factory
where his father and father's father had done the same.

At day's end, he'd return to us with their burdens,
their debts, drunk wives, deadbeat fathers, dead children,
for my mother to bear over drinks
while I removed myself to play in the nearby woods
until the silent dinner
and ignored he who'd laced my boots, bandaged my finger,
paid someone's else's bill,
knowing nothing of onus and its seclusions, its leaden quiet,
of the coming call, far in the future, to question my ancient hurts.

Do Not Rush the Wound to Mending

Do not rush the wound to mending
if the very act of caring is the cure;
what matters to the hurt is the tending.

Although most try to speed the pain to ending,
those who treat beneath the sore
do not rush the wound to mending.

The scathed ones, steadfast with pretending
to be fine, should be assured
what matters to the hurt is the tending.

Those who give refuge do it transcending
and, as they balm and soothe above the roar,
do not rush the wound to mending.

The brave bombed who suffer silent and unbending
should seclude and be sheltered, for
what matters to the hurt is the tending.

And you, the battered, into your grief descending,
rise into relief's embrace and endure.
Do not rush the wound to mending.
What matters to the hurt is the tending.

Haiku for a Rescued Barn

Unjoined by great age
softened, sunk, and slumped by rot
a brink of hope deemed

Bygone barn razing
averted: moved, grounded, saved
a phoenix in wood

Stripped, sheathed, clapboarded
old iron braces old beams
repurposed purpose

Poured light squared in panes
lofts aloft for space and air
held smell of beasts still

Unreined harness hangs
unswung scythe and pitchfork hung
objects of art now

Gone of grain and grist
making hay is different now
new fodder feeds us

New Wine

We sat in the grass at the edge of a pear orchard
and ate fig spread on baguettes so fine
that I was embarrassed by how pleased I was.

The tagalong college girl spread out before us
her catholic guilt,
insisted on a visit to the Palace of the Popes,
which the boys laughed off with a honeyed plan
to drink wine and meet local women
at the Beaujolais Nouveau wine festival
in the village square.

The girl and I went instead to the hollow palace
with differing intentions
and met them later to get the train for the coast.

They told of how carnal it was in the square
and how they'd been pulled into a grape-stomping contest
and that one of them won
and how the women, drunk on his victory,
licked the purple-pink juice from his feet and calves.

They said how warm and gracious the women were,
that they'd all known each other since they were schoolgirls.

I remember the tender way the boys recounted it,
but less about what the girls did with them
in the purple shade of the bistro umbrellas.

It is not the going instead to the voided palace
where time had left only the one smell
of something burning daily for millennia
that I regret.

It is not even the olive-skinned women
in their rapture loosening their dresses unbidden
or the claret sheen on their lips

that I wish was more than just a figment.

I regret missing the way the breeze made them feel
in the violet hour when they were done
and how it cooled them as they drank
and talked warmly of the day in the square.

Sisyphus Resting

What you would have said if you caught Sisyphus resting:
Of course. Finally. Good for you.
Or if you happened to pass by Achilles
during his preparations for battle:
Pardon me, but your heel is showing.

Your comments would have been rhetorical –
it was always up to them –
they picked their fights with fate.
But your words would have broken the ice.

What *was* he thinking
as he watched the rock roll away
that first time?
A feeling of freedom blunted
by the sudden understanding that he would
forever do it all over again.
Then that very lucidity placing him above his fate.
Then maybe some joy about the task to come,
the day laborer's flinted satisfaction
pocked with moments of melancholy
when he reflects on all that he left behind
or considers the futility of any wish at all.
Acceptance and resolve lower the resistance
of the boulder, make it slightly rounder.

Was there an instant of disbelief as the arrow pierced the skin?
Then a dawning as he watched his blood ebb into Troy's lava soil?
Perceiving himself for the first time.
At last seeing through the gasbaggery of his so-called compatriots,
how they fed him fruits that did not exist,
indulged his wrath addiction,
deflected concerns about his heel,
told his story grandstandingly when out of earshot,
as if it were their own.
Accepted that he was not departing a hero as he bled out,
but just arriving at his comeuppance.

You would have wanted to know
how deep their understanding went in those moments,
if they inferred that one cannot flaunt
scorn for the gods,
a hatred of death,
and a passion for life
and expect to get away with it.

BOMBMAKERS

We were bombmakers
in size 7 suede Pumas
working with pluck and fervor
in your father's garage.

Dissecting firecrackers with x-acto knives
for their scant gunpowder
was like expecting blood in the mice
we sliced open in science class.

We scraped the silver dust into a styrofoam cup
and added sawdust and anything else
that had *Flammable* written on it.
Then the jerry can gasoline,
that pyro's go-to, that sure thing.

The apple-red Bic lighter,
stolen from your mother,
who had trusted us and gone out for cigarettes,
serpent-licked the fuse.

The only explosion
our guilt:
nothing but flame
and its soundless promise to spread.

Your stamping sneakers spread it
from cup to pant leg,
like what always happens
when you pound a puddle.

Down you went in the grass rolling.
Out went the flame too late.
Up the driveway drove your mother.
From the window the cigarette.

To the hospital we went in the station wagon wayback,

our bare feet, pressed on the windows,
left footprint ghosts to haunt us
when it was all over.

All these years later, I wonder if
when you tell the scar's story
anyone understands how much was riding on the freedom
to alchemy destruction in a cup,
to earn a wound of our own making,
a symbol that got smaller over time
but no less permanent.

A HAND ON HIS SACHEM'S SHOULDER

after Stephen Vincent Benet

They came on to fish-hook Orleans in this way,
in this manner,
with their hulls over fallen weirs,
their trains over spits of sand,
past fields where the rye was high.
Cranberries grew and floated in the bogs,
oysters in their beds.
It was a rugged place giving up its plenty
in a fragile, tended peace with the wind and tides –
full of shingled windmills and saltworks,
fresh kettle ponds,
and farms with ducks as white as shadbush.

A farmer lived on a great bluff
with a steady wind that flumed cool
through his house.
He ran his mill from it
and ground corn into wide-mouthed sacks.
A Boston Brahmin stopped by there
to inquire as to the ocean view, to divine the value.
He was given cornmeal cakes from a skillet;
it was earthy and sweet in his mouth.
The dried mackerel was sweet to him, too.

He heard the cool wind's music
as the farmer's wife served him.
Remembering the *Mayflower* passengers
and their native friendships,
he ate and gazed at the sea
then drove off in his Model A
crushing the wild yard.
It was a thing he remembered
as long as any excavator flexing its muscle in the wind.

Place of sturdy, modest houses
and long slopes to Pleasant Bay,
broad-backed clam rakers and patient wiersmen,
whaler's women.
Where 49 Pilgrims came to found a steady town
among the Nausets,
and the packet ships of my ancestor's boyhood
later chugged up the tidal rivers
past the meetinghouse and the churches and the leaning elms.

Pilgrims stood under these trees
with painted sagamores beside them.
On Main Street, the market-women sold cod
fanned out like playing cards.
The apothecary's shelves brimmed
with green Pippin Apples and Battle Ax tobacco.
Dockside shuckers slipped quahogs from their cases
for eating raw,
the muddy shells a fading onyx,
their purpled insides wampum ready.

Scenes from *The Landing at Plimoth*
papered the ice-cream parlor.
The fish ran for months,
their schools on the surface and visible to the eye.
Miles Standish stood under his elm,
a hand on his sachem's shoulder,
the taste of gifted corn long gone from his mouth.
His gaze was restfully on God, but his wits and bargain fierce.

So I want to remember what the rememberers remembered.
The whir and whoosh
of spinning wheels and looms in the houses.
The goat bell sound
of quahog shells striking
the fir planks of decks and docks and market stalls
worn from boots.
The burning of those shells into lime.

The heavy stones
of the tide-water grist mills

in their summer grind at the harbor head
as dependable as the moon.

The plumped, golden seed heads
of bending barley,
the clay-orange road dust
on the windowpanes through summer,
and, in October, the stray cranberries
on the market floors,
and the red stain they left for a while.

So I want to remember you, teeming place
of broad-backed clammers,
cape of warm, shallow bays and farms with mills,
loose and locomotive in their turning.

And so they found you
with their ships carrying bibles and drawings of churches,
their blankets carrying smallpox,
their churches blanketing the town.
On and on it went over epochs and eras
cowing your people
with their beads and cholera, deeds and bank notes.

And they moved with such zeal against you so many times,
and you gave them skins and hides,
cornmeal in skillets,
sacred waterfront,
let them shuck the land.
You did deals with the seekers craving
what they could take from the wind and tides.

POISONING PABLO NERUDA

Scientists confirmed that he was injected with a bacteria that caused his death; lawyers accuse Pinochet's state agents.

He injected his readers with toxins,
      ideas about loves they could never have.
Trace amounts were found in their teeth and bones,
      in autopsies of their wanting hearts.
He abandoned his family,
      ravaged a servant girl in Ceylon,
            wrote dispassionately about it,
      poisoned himself with moral failings,
            became unread, unreadable.
The poet's true death.

A Short History of Failed Bridges

When I see rivers curving towards or away
cutting landscapes into two sides
I like to think of a first bridge builder
laying tree trunks, festooning vines.
Or of a Roman prodigy and his arches and beams.
In their minds,
those that were swept away.
Short histories of failed bridges.

How often have you known
that not bridging means not arriving,
yet built a flawed crossing
            or none at all
and started in the wrong place,
misread the tide
            of the moment,
mistook depths for shallows?

SAVING EELGRASS

Blind and chairbound is my aged mother
when I visit her with wounds freshly stitched.
She softly skims their braille with fine fingers
and makes her maternal inferences,
her sight line into my depths and shallows.

Deep under dark water is a meadow,
unseen acres of willowy green unsung –
no fluorescence of reefs in red and blue,
no eerie charisma of mangrove swamps.
Just a nursery for the progeny
     of the sea,
a shield for the shoreline from the wave's blow –
careworn from years of fluid indifference,
cut by anchor drag and propeller churn,
the blind tossing and fierce turning of things.

Hot murk sickens us with fall-out and run-off.
We wait in the opaque with diamond-scarce seeds
for the sun's mothering eye to light us,
for currents revived from rich beforetimes
to cool us down with riffling fingers,
to soothe and steady and coax us upward.

Poetry in the End

It's almost as if it was okay
when it all started going wrong
irreversibly,
because I knew there would be
poetry in the end.

For years, the right words
were always away on business
or pressed into other errands.
Writing someone else's books.
Crafting ellipses, shaping shells and pretty hollows.
Making a fetish of the unsaid.
Like that poem about the CIA operative writing to his son.

Sadness was too distracted to describe itself,
and grief avoided its name by spooling out too slowly to notice.
The way weeping happened when words weren't around,
and would've said the wrong thing even if they were.

I do not mean the music that thinking is to the mind,
that the heart need not hear, would never dance to.
There was plenty of that.
I mean the poetry of sounds I could not speak,
the mutes, aspirates, and liquids
where meaning flows and pools.

In an era before all of this,
in the aftermath of a calamity
I could not heal with words,
I sought silence in a Georgian farmhouse
on a hillside in Wales.
The innkeeper spooned cawl and bara brith into a simple bowl,
ladled the lyrical into everything she said.
I ate all of it not knowing what it was,
heard my mind being coaxed open

by the emeraldine of the fells and dales,
by fly fishing the River Vrynwy clumsily
but with purpose.
My creel was lined with moss, though remained empty.
A barman moved me deeply with Welsh words
that had no translation.
All I could receive was their sounds, rolling and guttural,
like an ornate ironwork door imploring its hinges
to sing of its own forging.

Even further back, in 1989,
making rice paper all day with that waif of a Japanese girl,
her 6th floor walk-up, the snow cycloning in nuances.
I don't remember what I labored to write on it,
but I do recall its dissolution
in the instant it touched our tongues.

And all the following years,
during those splendid days on Nauset
when the water and air were so perfect together
that all we could do was look up and out and nod.
But I wrote nothing of them,
nor of the love for my children despite how it brimmed.
Like a cargo ship gone missing,
but not yet written off.

Then finally feeling myself feeling.
Making it safe for the words to come back.
The chickadee that at last comes to my palm
for the single seed
because I had held it still long enough.
A noun shelled in a verb finding its flight.

Poetry to begin with.

WONDER

Ring the bells that still can ring
Forget your perfect offering
There's a crack in everything
That's how the light gets in
LEONARD COHEN

The Seal Rib Candelabra

There was elegance in the way
you lived out your gene's intent
sleekly, watchfully under the sea,
and there was nobility in your dying bluntly
according to the great shark's design.

Once the waves took possession of your body,
there was imminence in the turning of the cogs
that slow-rolled you onto the beach
and to me and my joinery.

I carted you inland and gave you a proper burial
so that the soil would unhinge your joints and frames
and unsplice your timbers
for the planned shoveling up,
for the building of an afterlife beyond your earthly purpose.

We reimagined the church of you.
Your skull's empty pulpit,
the unbraced pews of your forelimbs,
the fallen steeple of your spine.

From the broken communion of your vertebrae
we made a mobile of their wafered disks.
When they are received on the tongues of the westerly wind,
they chime and remind us of you.

From the arches and buttresses of your ribs
we assembled a 15-armed candelabra
and sanctified you with tall, white candles.

Water once held you lightly; you were the essence of lightness in it.
Now you are a holder of light at the dinner table,
the altar for talk about our day at the ocean's edge.

Bastille Moon

for Julie

Cranberry Lodge
circa July 14, 1973

The July night our mother sprung us
from bedtime,
that bastille of her own making.
Her guard let down by cocktails
and a moon's orange beckoning
bigger than any she could remember,
low and rising over the bay.

She could still bound then,
her shoes probably kicked off
so she could take the stairs by twos.

The bedroom we shared
with the peaked and beamed ceiling
for staring at after stories
and the open window
for not escaping through after lights out.

Then she's there in hushing silhouette.
The sudden freedom to follow her on tiptoes
past the deaf and dozing sentry, our grandmother.

The dark house alight with lunar rays
drawing shadows of the furniture in pen and ink.
The beach-facing door swung wide open,
a hatch to the moonscape.

One small step for a boy and a girl,
one giant leap for childhood,
and we are figures in that moonscape.
Almost floating above it now;

joy's zero gravity.

The lengths of low waves long down the shoreline
in a slow-motion whip to the jetty.
We three, arms locked and singing as we walk:
Left, left, left
my-wife-and-48-children-
on-the-verge-of-starvation-
without-any-gingerbread
did I do right, right, right.

The jetty's tiny craters filled by sea spray,
each pool lit up with its own moon.

The nobility of wonderment
that is every child's birthright.
The return to bed now forgotten
or never remembered.
The gift of uninhibited fullness,
a keepsake we give each other
simply by recalling it.

Things That Flew

A boy with a sapling cherry bow
and workshop twine
conspiring with bent bamboo garden stakes
and nails lashed to the ends for arrows
never quite struck the mourning doves,
who were so slow and close and plentiful on the ground,
the flying shaft obediently
warping away from its target
always a secret relief
because my grandfather
would make me eat what I killed

Safer to explain what the bees
did to me when I rousted them
from the cidered halls of the autumn's ground apples
drunk on their plunder and righteous,
my cost of satisfaction for
the point-blank shot

No punishment for that at home
only salve in a paste
of baking soda and vinegar

I was the merest of sparks,
some soft incandescent offshoot from a fire
in an updraft
colored by where it came from,
too young and small to last or set light to anyone or anything,
though the eye couldn't help but follow my jagged flight in the dark.

WHISK THE LIGHT

Only Van Gogh,
when he was far gone enough to know,

evaded that clear,
   unambiguous candor of atmosphere,
          in which everything has its due place
            and proportion
        and stands strictly where it is.

     Through a clinic window,
     his self spread outward to whisk the light,
     and the two agitated in unison,

in whorls and curls of color,
shadows troubling in wreaths,
    skies schooling in blue

   sbrushstrokes,
      and rippling from a thrown stone,
         from a wrong word dropped in his ear.

The mathematical structure of turbulent flow in paint.

           ~

I don't believe
               that his thick strokes of viridian
could solve for me the actual vineyard he paints.

    I don't believe
that his dabs of cadmium
could express the way it reflects vegetable precision

              in gnarled arches.
    I doubt he would see that it is a mirror

held up to a mirror,

with the object of the reflection
                    cambering and keeping its sharpness
                                        as it shortens out of sight.
                              Could he make float and shimmer
            - above its own exactness -
the meticulous, waist-high explosion of fruit

that envelops the vintner
as he marches
counting grapes and reckoning error?

If he and I were in the village, though,
                    he would convince me
with urgent fingerlings of color on jute
                    that these old women
                        were leaning out between shutters
                        and hovering over window boxes,

that the flesh was flapping on their upper arms
in time with their tongues
            and the dead-heading coaxes
of their fingers on blossoms.

                        ∾

He would look into the indiscriminate light,
                    and build frames around the open spaces,
reframe the closed ones.
He would reduce them to permanence,
                    return them to their connotations.

LEAVING TRACES

I am writing to tell you
I left traces in your ear
when you were a baby.

I whispered *Nauset* over and over
when I gently enclosed you with the harbor of my body
and floated you on all of my arms.

Later, I put wind and anchorage into the word
when I spoke it
as I threw you in the air
and again when I caught you.

All I wanted was for you to feel gladness,
unaccountably,
later in life
when anyone spoke of that hewn and golden elbow
jabbed into the rib of the sea
where dunes still rise and ships once sank,
each time nearly recollecting something
necessary that was missing.

THE MEANWHILE

I am driving the back country lanes of Vermont
on New Year's Day
and looking out at a new skin of powder and glaze,
an amnesty for the landscape,
its blots and blights under a forgiveness of white.

In the back, my three daughters are talking about *Little Women*
and how they simply could not go on
if they lost a sister to a weakened heart,
that uttered sentiment a sudden snowfall
over my own weakened one
and the cracked picket of bones around it,
a liniment of whiteness in words.

When exactly what you want is here,
live entirely in the meanwhile.
Do not wish for the present,
or the lanes of its mystery,
to end.

GRAINING YOUR VOICE

When you finally come to my door
having heard the great horned owl halloo
and the addict's plea on the train
and seen the coyote silk its way through
the yellowing field in the rain,

when you have watched the steam plume from the factory stack
and studied the redtail hawk wheeling
in a monoxide updraft over the highway
and the drunk reeling
in his bitter ballet,

and had your heart pulped by wickedness
and repaired to swollen by goodness
and become fluent in silence,

I will listen
to the miles told by the action of your gait,
to the past wringing of your still hands,
to the earned quiet of your eyes,
to the timbre graining your voice.

THE CABINED STAR

Apricity

The quitting sun,
on its way out in the days before the winter solstice,
low-angled and thinned from the axial tilt
    and unstopped by all that was green and now gone,
bares the bone structure of the vast salt marsh,
    its shoulder and neck, the beach's back,
alters how we perceive color and light,
    where it has come from and gone,
signals something idle beneath,
    some sleeping glow, tincts and hues bedded down,
like it can only come from the inside,
emissions from particles,
remnants turned omens,
attestations of a coming return

from a thousand gulls up high in constellations
flashing white from their wings,

from the waves with their manes blowing back, flowing white,
their hooves thundering the shoreline to white foam,

from the seagrasses in their millions
thrusting golden spears into the gray,

even at night, from the lone lobster boat's own cabined star
a burst of a white bloom in the black.

Two Bays

All water has a perfect memory
and is forever trying to get back to where it was.
— Toni Morrison, *Beloved*

Yes to the bay as water
and to that bay
when it is two bays
one in June and one in September
the warming and cooling ceding sway to the other

Yes to the shoreline and the bottom
the memory of where the water has been
the foretellers of where it will be

Yes to the bay's two selves
water and basin
one is flow and drama
the other
purpose
that is the one to know

Yes to what happens when that water brightens
and the sunlight off its skin rinses
and the being and seen feeling
in those moments

Yes to finally revealing the difference between
being brought to life by moonlight standing in the field
and standing here now in the farmhouse kitchen
with skin hued by the flickering
of all those candle flames

Both of me

NECTAR RISING

To thrive, a meadow must maintain an open character.
— The Journal of Meadow Management (Vol XIX, Spring 1949)

If you watch long and closely enough,
you will see the meadow slowly turning itself
into a place for shelter from it all,
beckoning the wind to bring what will stay,
coaxing the soil to keep it,
staying supine to the rain,
sweet-talking the sun into its endmost vision of shade.

The meadow's buried and reaching heart,
the siphon and pump of change,
will swell roots with tissue and pith
and pressure their interlacing span to absorb,
will inspirit liquid up into narrow spaces,
nectar up stamen,
water up stalks and stems
that want to be structures of wood.
The field's vascular schema,
its ducts and vessels,
its capillaries of intent
at last delivering its meaning in lasting stands and copses,
where change is lastingly slight.

Something in me needs to be under crown and canopy,
to limit what light can betray,
to shadow my understory,
to choose the beaten paths and usual trails of the deer and coyote
over the caprice of the birds in flight in the wide, blue clear,
to choose crouching in groves
among the blowdown and windthrow,
the nests and burrows,
over standing in acres of grasses in their flat and open sameness.

But something in me needs clearing,

to perform the ritual of opening
so that the sleeve of the wind with my heart out on it
can pulse the grasses as it passes undisturbed.
Something in me needs
a place for light to beat unblocked and to bathe extravagantly,
to bare and shed.
Something in me needs
an unbroken plane for perspectives to fan out in lines of sight,
vacant of other agendas,
right up to wherever the edges are,
to where stasis creates itself on purpose.
Where woodland meets grassland, say.
Where one way of being accommodates another.
You and me, say. Us and them.
Where light falls fully yet and dark falls darkly.
No dapples or patches of umbra.

There is no clearing without cutting,
no opening without the slash and slice,
even when the reaping is just air and light.
When the fodder is only space.
When it is simply the granting
of goldenness to the goldenrod to beguile the rabbit,
of blueness to the cornflower to flirt the bee,
of cosmic intricacy to the Queen Anne's Lace,
its thousand tiny white flowers in a fretwork
uniting to latch a single seed to a feather,
or to trust the sole inkling of its future self to a beetle,
or to drop its jewel in the switchgrass and little bluestem
where the beginnings of the blackhaw are,
where the soil's heart siphons and pools the carbon
away from us,
its harms sequestered.

It is the act of keeping open at the right time –
whenever your seasons tell you.
In a meditative pattern of cuts,
start at the center and work your way out in straight rows
to the edges
so that the nectar will rise again
and give of itself.

CREATION

Sixty seconds were epiphanic.
Your clothing of language was stripped from you;
there was no climate for it where you went.
The one-hundred twenty-nine words that followed
were hollow,
were pointless cairns,
doused pyres lined up
on a dimming shoreline.
You floated then drifted,
but with extreme precision
and without moving.
Your heltering thoughts
skeltered against each other in passing,
hulls glancing icebergs.
The friction smelled
like books burning
in the corridors between nanoseconds.
Then the elation of landfall
without having left,
where the percussion of atoms forming
and the vibration of their covalent bonding
echoed in each of your three trillion pores
each with its own voice that you recognized.
Ninety miles down
you wore the earth's mantle briefly
for a billion years
as keeper of the fahrenheit,
applier of the pressure,
erupter of magma
until every word you formed
tumbled from the kimberlite of your lips
a diamond.

QUILTING THE BAY

for Chloë

The moon and the winter in kinship
are making a wedding quilt to cover the bay.
The tides let the ice form and stay;
the ice forgives the ebb and flow in courtship.

Frost flowers bloom white in fine feathers,
Starburst cracks radiate outward
       from a point where a gull dropped a quahog.
Fractals connect in jagged geometries.

I need symbols in the patchwork design,
stories on the frozen fabric,
beauty in the union of form and function,

while the mallards thread the thawed edge's hem,
and a heron needles the open seam
to get what they need.

East Coast Low

We ignored the authorities' warnings
to stay off the roads of Barnstable County
and drove the truck through the swell of the tidal rivers
to the surge of the sea along the Nauset shore
that January day when the wind and water
and ice and snow frenzied away the light
in a dervish of northerly and southerly, in an ecstasy of air.

We were sure that the shorebirds had hunkered on the inlet side
and that the seabirds knew to gyre into the storm center
and break out to safety in the calmness of the eye.
We were there to look it in the eye
and kept moving to move with the strangeness
of the movement of air and water and white,
to watch it cover and carve the known with roil and rage,

to run from, yet towards, the chance it could blow us open
and take back what was ours,
go where we had been.

Love is a Crow

Long ago,
in the early days of discovering each other
we found that we both
admired the crow
for his graphic qualities,
for how splendidly he portrays on paper
in pen and ink,
in poems.

We imagined having one of our own
to delight in his tricks
and the oddments he gathers,
to marvel when he omens rain,
portends change,
embodies a soul
in his feathered blackness.

But now I'm drawn to the verb of him.

Let's crow
about the shiny thing
we've found and kept,
about our plumage
lustrous and iridescent,
about the we
of you and me.

LOVE IS AN OWL

Love is an owl when she flies
buoyant and exquisitely slow in flight
dependent on her own hush
and providence

alights on a place with a view
her eyes round high windows
tawny in the paling sun
open to all that moves her

her face turned to channel the sound
of a heart beating
so that she knows
exactly where I am

EREMITION

This is the means by which we,
who are ordinarily set into motion by things,
become able to set things into motion.
— Dōgen Zenji

He finally stopped the making,
became the stone that the builder refuses,
and said
I am made

left the shipping to the tides
and said
I am oceans

returned time to the wheeling sun
and said
My days and nights are yours

aimed the long lens of patience
at his deep space,
his quantum,
discovered a stillness,
its new laws of movement golden

got a dog to learn the cosmos of joy,
a guitar for the cosmos in its cords
latent until he learns them,
the big bang behind their vibrating strings,
the god mix of physics and music

where there are no answers
because there are no questions

ABOUT THE AUTHOR

A former academic turned partner at Bain & Company, Gregory
LeStage brings discipline, grit, and clarity to both his professional life
and his poetry. When not writing, he devotes himself to hands-on
restoration projects—rescuing an 1810 Cape Cod barn from demoli-
tion, rebuilding the cab of a 1949 Chevy farm truck by hand, coaxing a
1962 Vietnam-era Dodge M37 back to life, or or keeping a 1940 Farmall
tractor running. His love for old tools, enduring things, and work done
slowly by hand informs both his writing and his way of being.

LeStage holds a PhD and Master's from Oxford University and a BA
from Trinity College. His poems have appeared in numerous publica-
tions, and his first collection, *Small Gods of Summer*, was a finalist for
the Eric Hoffer Prize and his second, *Hope Is a Small Barn*, was a runner
up for the Julia Ward Howe Prize. Whether in a workshop or at the
page, he works with what he has: memory, imagination, and the desire
to connect. For him, poetry is no different than carpentry or restoration
—it's about joining one word to another in a way that might hold.

About J.P. Zenger Books

JPZENGERBOOKS.COM

We publish books that deserve to exist.

We're a small, independent imprint dedicated to bringing forward works that might otherwise go unheard—ideas that challenge, stories that resonate, voices that endure. Our focus is simple: publish books that matter, with the care and conviction they deserve.

We seek to bridge the divide between poets and the broader reading public. We believe that poetry should not be confined to the academy or limited to insular literary circles—it should be vibrant, accessible, and alive in the daily consciousness of readers everywhere. Our mission is to publish and promote poetry that speaks across boundaries: of class, geography, culture, and experience. Whether encountered in a neighborhood bookstore, heard on a podcast, or discovered through a shared link on social media, we aim to place poetry where it belongs: in the hands and hearts of readers.

We are committed to publishing work that surprises, moves, and endures. J.P. Zenger Books seeks manuscripts that demonstrate artistic excellence, emotional honesty, and linguistic precision. Our editorial vision embraces diversity—in voice, theme, and form. We welcome poets from all backgrounds, and we actively seek work that challenges conventions and reflects the full range of contemporary life.

www.ingramcontent.com/pod-product-compliance
Lightning Source LLC
Chambersburg PA
CBHW051642120626

46551CB00015B/2186